Handle
stress

*Learn how to manage your stress
and take charge of yourself*

GW00394282

Kate Keenan

Pocket
Manager
Books

Published by Pocket Manager Books
www.pocketmanagerbooks.com

ISBN (Print)   978-1-909179-46-2
ISBN (eBook) 978-1-909179-59-2
ISBN (Pdf)   978-1-909179-73-8

A CIP catalogue record for this book is available from the
British Library.

Previously published as 'The Management Guide to Handling Stress'
by Oval Books, 1998, 2002.

Original series editor – Anne Tauté, Oval Books
Editor – Catriona Tulloch Scott
Project manager – Clare Christian, The Book Guru
Book and cover re-design – Philip Jansseune, Walker Jansseune
Image enhancement – Matt Holland, MiH Design
Author photograph – Marko Dutka, Studio Marko

*Cover – Undoing the knot in stress is easier than you think. All it
takes is a bit of effort.*

Contents

This book is dedicated to
those who would like to manage better
but are too busy to begin.

To download your **FREE** Workbook
which accompanies
Handle stress

please visit:

**www.pocketmanagerbooks.com/books/
handle-stress**

Handle stress

Everyone is under stress. But not all stress is the kind that impairs your performance. If it was, there would be no mountaineers or deep-sea divers, people who thrive on stress. The important difference is that they can handle the stress, because they have chosen to take control of the circumstances in which they experience it.

In everyday life, stress usually takes the form of mental or physical tension which you would rather not have. At work, this generally boils down to the pressures to get things done, and at home family, worries can often keep you awake at night. It is when these forces become too great that you can feel out of control, and frequently are. This is because stress affects your ability to think clearly and clouds your judgement.

It will help to stop pressure from becoming too stressful if you can first recognise the symptoms of stress and then know how to take preventative action. Fortunately it is never too late to start.

This book helps you understand how stress could be affecting your life and offers you practical and powerful ways of handling it.

1 The need to handle stress

Stress is the natural reaction you have to excessive pressure. The rapid pace of life today, along with increased expectations and time constraints, means that everyone has to tolerate more pressure now than ever before.

This means that you can easily get used to living with stress, and strive to meet ever-increasing amounts of work, while at the same time wondering why you do not seem able to get the pleasure out of life that you once did. It is important to realise that stress is a condition that needs to be handled positively.

Sort the good stress from the bad

For most people, the term 'stress' usually has negative associations. But in fact, there are two kinds, good and bad.

- **Good stress** or 'eu-stress'. To get the most out of your life you need some 'good stress' to act as an impetus when meeting challenges. The technical term for this stress is 'arousal'. You need to be sufficiently aroused to get out of bed and go to work. As the day goes on, you become more alert until you reach your optimum performance, which is when you do your best work. When you are in control of your stress levels, you enjoy the challenges which play an integral part in achieving your aims.

- **Bad stress** or 'dys-stress'. This results in feeling that the pressures in your life have become overwhelming and you are no longer able to cope. It is this type of stress that people really mean when they say they are 'stressed'. If this condition is left unresolved, bad stress can escalate from a feeling of being snowed under to becoming physically ill and psychologically distressed.

Whether good stress becomes bad stress will very much depend on both your individual circumstances and personal qualities and strengths. The onset of 'dys-stress' can be sudden and dramatic, and is sometimes prompted by a specific incident. But for many people the effects of stress tend to be relentless and cumulative, as skills for coping with life gradually degenerate and the ability to function positively declines.

This need not be an inexorable process. If you can recognise the early signs of stress, you can begin to do something to counteract its effects.

Signs of stress

The clue as to whether you could be succumbing to stress is being able to spot any negative changes in your behaviour. Sometimes these can be difficult to spot. But some of the more common signs that indicate that you might be experiencing stress can include:

- Getting ratty with people and over-reacting at the least problem of difficult situation.
- Having less energy than usual and so achieving less.
- Being more argumentative and quibbling about things which would normally be acceptable.
- Needing a drink to get going.
- Feeling persistently miserable and gloomy.
- Having a sense of being out of control: of being swamped by demands – all of which need to be addressed and carried out at the same time.
- Experiencing unwelcome physical reactions such as a racing heart, a churning stomach, sweating, shivering, headaches and skin rashes.

It is easy to think these responses may be due to life just being more difficult than it used to be; or that because circumstances are constantly changing it is impossible to keep pace with events so there is not much point in even trying. In fact, such reasoning is symptomatic of someone working under stress.

Negative strategies

When people are stressed, they may often adopt strategies which they think will alleviate their discomfort. Unfortunately, these are more often negative than positive. Typically, the negative of things you might find yourself doing if you are stressed can include:

- Running away and ignoring a problem or pretending that there is no problem at all; denying that anything is wrong and declaring, when asked, that everything is fine, although it is obvious to everyone else that it is not.
- Fretting or brooding over your worries and their consequences without having the energy to take any action to change them.
- Vacillating and dithering between one decision and another because you fear committing to a definite course of action.
- Procrastinating by diverting your energies from the job in hand by engaging in delaying tactics, doing anything rather than making a start.
- Seeking excitement and doing reckless things as a short-term distraction to feeling dispirited.
- Venting emotions and erupting in anger, making stinging remarks, or bursting into tears as a release for feelings of exasperation, agitation and disquiet.
- Becoming a couch-potato and withdrawing from taking part in activities which formerly you would have found interesting and engaging.

Such strategies involve you doing things which are not only unproductive but can also make you feel even more stressed in the long run. They are often an unconscious manifestation of trying to rid yourself of pent-up feelings, but in reality they simply create further stress.

Focus on handling stress positively

You are likely to feel stressed when the pressures around you exceed your abilities to cope. In addition, you may not be aware that the discomfort you are feeling is stress. Nor may you realise that if you could correctly identify the signs, you could do something about it.

One of the critical manifestations of stressful behaviour is that you adopt totally inappropriate ways of dealing with it. And paradoxically, the methods you may choose are likely to precipitate more stress rather than reduce it.

Not all stress is debilitating. Good stress activates mechanisms which help you to cope with challenging circumstances. But bad stress is an insidious condition which requires you to understand it if you are going to be able to handle it positively.

Questions to ask yourself

Think about what has been happening to you in the past few weeks and consider how you would answer the following questions:

- Have I found myself recently over-reacting to fairly trivial events and situations?

- Am I finding it difficult to make even the most simple decision?

- Do I seem to be always tired for no discernable reason?

- Do I think I have too much to cope with?

- Do I tend to ignore problems in the vain hope that they will go away?

- Do I delay facing up to issues and problems?

- Am I incessantly turning things over and over in my mind with no conclusion or productive outcome?

If you have answered 'Yes' to many or all of these questions, you may well be demonstrating some typical signs of 'dys-stress' and need to do something about ridding yourself of them.

You will be doing better if…

- You appreciate that there is a difference between good stress and bad stress.

- You realise that bad stress is a direct reaction to an inability to cope with excessive pressure.

- You recognise that adverse symptoms, such as lack of energy, putting things off, excessive introspection, irritability and explosive behaviour are all signs that you may be suffering from stress.

- You are aware that adopting negative strategies is probably not the most effective way to handle stress in the long-term.

- You acknowledge that pretending that problems do not exist will not make your stress disappear.

- You understand that not handling your stress positively can only make you more stressed than ever.

2 Understand stress

Understanding the intricate nature of stress is the first step in the process of handling it proactively.

The stress response

The physical reaction to stress has been programmed in human beings since prehistoric times. It is the basic survival instinct which involves a complex sequence of physiological responses to warding off a 'perceived' threat. When stone-age man came face to face with a hairy mammoth, he perceived this as a threat. His brain signalled fright and prepared his body to deal with the emergency by mobilising it for one of two courses of action:

- **Fight** This means confronting the aggressor.
- **Flight** This means running away as fast as possible.

While the threats which you face in modern life may not be quite the same, your response to them is.

Battle stations to the body

When the brain interprets a situation as alarming, the hypothalamus, the 'stress centre' in the brain, triggers a number of internal systems in the body, as if readying it for battle. These are:

- **The sympathetic nervous system** This system releases adrenaline into the blood stream, which increases both the heart rate and blood pressure, the two key things which stimulate the state of arousal required to provide a quick energy fix to prepare you for action. The problem is that this life-saving process drains the blood from the brain and therefore its oxygen supply. As oxygen is necessary for the brain to function rationally, this explains why people can find themselves freezing or doing something irrational when in threatening situations.
- **The endocrine system** This system releases the body's 'major stress hormone', adrenocorticotrophic hormone (ACTH), which increases the glucose levels in the blood thus fuelling the muscles to respond positively to the emergency. This means that the body is fully primed to act, either to fight or run away from the threat, and this explains why people can do superhuman things when they are in danger.

All this activity gears the body to protect itself. As the breathing rate increases, the body's natural painkillers, the endorphins, are activated. More red blood cells are released to help carry oxygen to feet and hands and more white corpuscles are produced to fight infection should an injury occur.

If the threat is of an immediate kind, such as a near-fatal accident, once you get out of danger the body begins the calming down process. Once the stressful event is over, the reaction to the emergency subsides and the parasympathetic nervous system takes over, returning the body to its normal state.

Prolonged stress reactions

However, if the threat has been present for a while and involves prolonged tension, such as spending days preparing for a speech, the body tends to take much longer to come back into a balanced state once the event has taken place. If the threat is a constant menace, the kind experienced when meeting endless and ever-increasing demands over a long period of time, your body's call to 'battle stations' is not able to let up. You are unable to relax or feel comfortable. This is because the ACTH stress hormone is continuously being activated and you therefore never get a chance to revert to a harmonious state.

If, through persistent pressure, your defence system stays on constant alert, it could eventually fail you from sheer exhaustion. Intense physiological arousal of this sort which extends over a very long period can be extremely debilitating and ultimately harmful.

Although the body begins to recover from the initial alarm-reaction, the blood glucose levels become dangerously low. Your body's resources become depleted and you become more susceptible to physical disorders such as heart disease, high blood pressure, asthma or even the common cold. Therefore, the earlier you take positive action to break the cycle or to change your situation, the better.

Shell shock to the brain

Most modern-day situations which cause you stress are not so extreme that they require you to take the fight or flight option. In any case, in most circumstances, neither action would be appropriate. The main problem is that the brain is not able to tell the difference between a serious life-threatening situation, such as facing up to a hairy mammoth, or an unwelcome disturbance, such as a personality clash at work.

Regardless of the cause, the age-old stress response to what the mind interprets as a threat is set in motion. Within seconds, adrenaline is charging round your system and which, if not given a physical outlet, will produce a state of mental fluster accompanied by physical reactions such as churning sensations in the stomach, sweaty palms, pounding heart, dry mouth and weak limbs. Your body has instinctively primed itself for action, when what you really need is a raised level of rational thinking to temper that instinct. Unfortunately all this physical disturbance has a dire effect on the thinking processes, the most common being:

- **Not being able to think straight** You can find it hard to organise your thoughts logically so that you can tackle problems. Feeling frazzled often leads you to doubt your own competence.
- **Being easily distracted** You can find it difficult to concentrate and as a result, your performance tends to deteriorate. A lack of concentration and focus leads to difficulty in completing tasks.
- **Behaving in a more extreme way** You can find yourself adhering rigidly to established patterns of behaviour and being blinkered to alternatives. This leads to an incapacity to adapt when circumstances change and flexible responses are required.

The inability to think objectively about a situation makes it more difficult to cope in a constructive way. But once you know the effect that stress can have on your reasoning abilities, it is much easier to take remedial action.

The chain reaction

Because your body and mind are inextricably linked, it is your initial appraisal of a situation which triggers the physical chain reaction and this determines the intensity of your emotional response. When you interpret a certain situation as exciting and exhilarating, such as when an event is demanding but manageable, the body's alarm system gives you the positive stimulus to take action and allows you to enjoy achieving your objective. But if you interpret a situation as intimidating and upsetting, such as when work escalates and you are already working at full stretch, a state of paralysing stress can often be the result.

Feelings do not arise out of the blue; they result from your perceptions. It is from your thoughts that your feelings, and ultimately your ensuing behaviour arise. It follows, therefore, that if you allow your initial thoughts to start out as negative or 'faulty', in that you may not have objectively appraised the situation and can only see the worst side of things, you can easily feel jumpy, grumpy, or just plain miserable, all of which will almost certainly cause you to behave in a stressed way.

Stressed feelings which remain unrelieved can often result in one or other of the following long-term psychological conditions:

- **Anxiety** When fears become unrealistic and out of all proportion in relation to the situation you are coping with, anxiety can easily set in. Some of the symptoms can include a sense of helplessness, a feeling that there is nothing you can do, panicky reactions, nervousness, jumpiness, an incapacity to concentrate and an inability to relax or to sleep.
- **Aggression** When efforts to achieve a goal are frustrated, aggression can be the result. Moods can become more volatile and swing violently backwards

and forwards at the drop of a hat. Symptoms may include becoming extremely irritable, short-tempered and over-reacting to trivial problems, along with demonstrating quarrelsome and bullying behaviour.

- **Depression** When worries become exaggerated or seem out of proportion, life may not appear to hold many attractions, and depression may take hold. Symptoms may include excessive tiredness and significant loss of energy, a total loss of purpose, excessive lethargy, weepiness, along with a sense of worthlessness and a feeling that life seems no longer worth living.

These can be some of the psychological consequences if you experience stress over a long period of time and sadly, if you do nothing, these conditions only tend to become progressively worse.

So before such reactions to stress become a way of life, you need to begin to identify those sources of stress which may be causing your lack of mental equilibrium. Once you have gained an insight into the sorts of situations that can cause stress, you can begin to identify the types of events or thoughts that tend to upset you and cause you to become stressed. And once you have identified these, you can begin to unravel the chain reaction because you are now more aware of the sorts of reactions you are likely to experience.

Atavistic responses

Because the brain still responds to threat in the same way as it did when stone-age man walked the earth, you need to be aware of your own emotional responses to any given situation. It is your interpretation of whether or not something is threatening which determines the degree to which you feel stressed.

These atavistic responses are still as primitive as they were when human beings were hunter-gatherers. You would have thought that they would have evolved between the Stone Age and the age of the Internet – but this is not the case. Modern human beings are not well adapted to modern life. Once you have some understanding of the nature of stress, it is easy to see why.

Questions to ask yourself

Think about how you view stress and ask yourself the following questions:

- Do I appreciate that the purpose of the 'fight or flight' response is to help maximise my survival?

- Do I understand that when the brain senses there is a threat present it automatically gears the body to protect itself?

- Do I recognise that feeling stressed can prevent me from thinking straight?

- Do I appreciate that prolonged stress depletes the body's resources, making it more susceptible to illness?

- Do I appreciate that prolonged stress may also result in making me feel anxious and/or depressed?

- Do I realise that it is when I interpret a situation as threatening that the body's alarm system is then triggered?

You will be doing better if…

- You appreciate that the brain still responds to threatening situations in exactly the same way as it did in prehistoric times.

- You realise that the body activates defence mechanisms to protect itself when it feels threatened.

- You understand that the body cannot return to a balanced state while the mind is on 'red alert'.

- You are aware that a long-term background fear is more difficult to recover from than an immediate frightening experience which concludes quickly.

- You understand that continuous feelings of stress can result in anxiety, aggression and depression.

- You appreciate that your logical thought processes can be significantly impaired by stress.

- You realise that it is how you perceive a situation that directly determines how you react to it.

3 Pinpoint your stressors

When you are feeling stressed, you rarely have the capacity to think about why this is so, you just know that you not feeling your usual self. Being able to put your finger on what exactly is causing you stress, commonly known as stressors, enables you to deal with them more successfully. Once you can do this you will also recognise that stressors usually turn up of their own accord, with no prompting from you. In general, stressors tend to derive from three key sources:

- **Your own intrinsic drivers** These have to do with the innate compulsive forces which motivate you to push yourself in certain ways, sometimes to excess.
- **Workplace pressures** These have to do with the strain you experience when carrying out your tasks in situations where constraints and demands can conspire to prevent your optimum performance.
- **Life events** These comprise the occasions, such as bereavement, divorce, debt or changing circumstances, which may push you to the limits of your capabilities and can sometimes cause you to re-evaluate significantly how your manage your life.

Stressors can be all-pervasive. They arise at any time and can leave you feeling exhausted and out of control.

Intrinsic drivers

Compulsive driving forces motivate your working style and affect everything you do. The way work is organised, time is managed, or personal relations are conducted are all subject to these drivers. When you are not under stress these can be highly effective and enhance performance. But when you are feeling stressed, they can drive your behaviour to extremes. There are five basic drivers which compel people in their working lives.

- **Urgency** With this driver, you are compelled to get a lot done in a short time. You respond particularly well to short deadlines and your energy and output peak under pressure. When you are not under stress, your strength is that you can achieve an enormous amount of work. But when you are feeling stressed, you tend to try to get even more done in an even more limited time, so you find that you have less opportunity to prepare and inevitably make more mistakes.
- **Perfection** This driver compels you to achieve perfection, demanding that you meet exacting personal standards. But under stress, you can end up not trusting anyone else to do things as well as you can, so you inevitably become swamped with work. You are also likely to misjudge the standard that is required and may spend time being unnecessarily absorbed by more and more detail.

- **Pleasing people** With this driver you aim to please without being asked and try to anticipate people's needs in advance by working out what would be required and providing it. But under stress you can over-anticipate and inadvertently antagonise others. You can become over-sensitive, or get upset if you feel your attempts to help have not been appreciated.
- **Trying hard** This driver compels you to put enormous effort into a task in your desire to achieve. You tackle things enthusiastically, and are prepared to take on all and sundry. But under stress you can easily take on too much, so that you end up accomplishing less and less and using up more and more energy.
- **Being strong** This is the driver that compels you to be strong at all times and you feel motivated when you are required to cope with high levels of pressure. You are extremely good at dealing with stressful situations and are very useful to have around in a crisis. But under stress you never ask for help and struggle on alone whatever the personal cost. Because you are so capable, people are always surprised when you fail.

Most people find it relatively easy to recognise that they may be motivated by one or more of these driving forces. There is not much you can really do to change them since, by their very nature, they are part of your nature.

But if you are aware of your personal drivers, you will be

able to recognise from your own behaviour the point at which they are becoming exaggerated and counter-productive. You can then try to tone them down, in much the same way as you would turn down the volume of a radio that is too loud.

Workplace pressures

Feeling continuously pressured at work without taking the time to analyse why this is so can add hugely to that pressure. Most people accept that a certain amount of stress 'goes with the job'. But if you are able to pinpoint those sources of work-related stress which are frequently accepted as natural, yet which are not, this will go a long way towards helping you handle and resolve them. Some of the main primary sources of workplace pressures are:

- **Impossible standards** Coping with impossible standards which have been set within an unrealistic timescale means that things are rarely completed. As soon as the demands made on you exceed your capabilities and resources, excessive stress inevitably arises. For example, if you are working long hours and have too much to do in the time allotted or if your work is problematic and not clearly defined, you will end up feeling fraught and exhausted.
- **Constant changes** Working in constantly changing circumstances means that the unexpected can become

the norm. If you are unsure of your own area of responsibility or there is no clear picture of what is expected of you, feelings of apprehension and demotivation will often tend to result.

- **Job insecurity** Experiencing job insecurity leaves you feeling unsure and fearful of what the future holds. This can produce severe anxiety which in turn reduces performance and can produce mood swings from bravura to the depths of depression.
- **A personality clash** Working with a disagreeable person can mean that your own and other people's finer feelings are overridden. This will often result in lowered performance and feelings of frustration and tension, along with personal antagonism.
- **Too much responsibility** Taking on too much responsibility causes the buck to stop with you far too often. This pressure can often result in your having difficulties in making decisions, along with a significant loss of concentration.
- **A heavy workload** Having too heavy a workload may mean you have far too much to do in the time allocated or that you are no longer good at setting priorities. The resulting pressure may cause you to become erratic and frantic, which creates even more work for you.

In most of these circumstances, you are reacting to pressures which are rarely of your own making. This leaves you feeling that you are less in control of what you have to do, leading you down the self-defeating spiral of stress, a fall in standards, an increase in grievances, a heightened sense of failure and, inevitably, more stress.

By taking a little time to appraise your working life as soon as you begin feeling unusually pressurised enables you to pinpoint the causes of potential stress which may be bubbling up. The process of doing this provides relief because you will now have some idea about from where the stress may be originating. It also means you will not be adding to your stress levels by thinking that, somehow, you are to blame for all this.

Life events

Encountering innumerable changes and difficulties, ups and downs, is so much a part of life that you may have accepted levels of stress which are, in fact, unacceptable, rather in the same way as a sailor adapts to the rolling deck of a ship. Because of this, it is useful to try to identify the issues in your personal life which may also be underlying causes of your stress.

Major life events

The death of a close relative, marital separation, personal injury or illness, are obviously stressful event in anyone's life. These may take time to recover from, but they are clearly identified as events which are likely to cause stress and pain. However events that are not sad or painful, such as getting married or moving house, can also cause stress. This is because you are required to make substantial personal adjustments and come to terms with a new situation which, however desirable, will make a considerable impact on your life overall, and thus can cause stress.

Day-to-day aggravations

While you expect to feel stressed when you experience a major event in your life, much of this will be eased in time. But the kind of aggravations you experience on a daily basis (such as encountering a regular traffic jam or being constantly interrupted when you are trying to concentrate) do not fade away. They occur incessantly. No sooner do you deal with one when another takes its place. This can cause you much more stress than you may realise as your inner resources can end up being depleted because of the constant demands being made on them.

Ageing

Adapting to mental and physical changes at different ages is more demanding than you might think, and can be a source of stress, especially at the mid-life point when hormones reduce, in men from around the age of thirty-five onwards, and in women from their late forties. This can have a direct effect on your physical well-being and behaviour, and may include some loss of short-term memory and reduced levels of energy.

All these various stressors are part of life's rich tapestry, and therefore you probably see these as circumstances you feel you should be able to cope with. But what you need to realise is that virtually any change in life requires you to adapt, and that this in itself can be a cause of stress.

The many sources of stress

It is important not to underestimate the effect that an accumulation of stressors can play in undermining people's ability to manage your stress. It is not the magnitude of one stressor or another that does this, but the cumulative effect. If these stressors arrived one at a time, you could probably handle them all quite easily. But when you have to deal with several and various stressors at the same time, this can generate a feeling of overpowering stress and often helplessness. Because these are concurrent, they constitute a barrage from which there may seem to be little or no escape.

Initially, it may appear that you are coping reasonably well with the combination of demanding personal drivers, workplace pressures and stressful life-events. However, the amount of effort required to do this slowly depletes your energy banks and therefore reduces your resilience.

The effect of this is that later changes may occur in your physical health when your ability to resist other stressful situations has been significantly reduced and this may bring about an extreme form of mental stress known as 'burnout'.

Begin remedial action

Stress can come from many sources, from external events not of your making, to internal drivers which form part of your personality and drives.

Identifying your individual compulsions can help you to become more aware of the way you function and how your behaviour can become more pronounced when you are under stress. It is also helpful to realise that a conjunction of pressures in your life and work can build up, like lava in a volcano, to produce all-engulfing stress.

Once you have pinpointed the events and areas of your life which are causing you stress, you are in a position to begin to take remedial action and reduce some of their potentially damaging effects.

Questions to ask yourself

Think about how drivers, workplace pressures and life events may affect both how you perform and the way you behave, and consider your answers to the following questions:

- Can I identify which specific drivers tend to motivate my behaviour?

- Can I recognise when these drivers seem to be getting out of control?

- Can I diagnose the particular workplace pressures which may be causing me stress?

- Do I realise that major events which are pleasant can cause just as much stress as sad and unhappy events?

- Do I accept that constant daily hassles can also account for a great deal of stress?

- Do I understand that an accumulation of stressors can create considerably more stress than the sum of these individual stressors?

You will be doing better if…

- You resolve to appraise your life in order to pinpoint those aspects that are potential stressors.

- You are more aware of the specific drivers that govern your behaviour.

- You can sense when your drivers may be going into overdrive.

- You realise how certain pressures at work can lead to feeling stressed.

- You recognise that continuous daily aggravations draw on your inner reserves more than you perhaps realised.

- You understand that positive events may be just as stressful as the ones which are more difficult to bear.

- You are aware that it is the cumulative effect of all your stressors, not necessarily very stressful in themselves, that can cause you to feel excessively stressed.

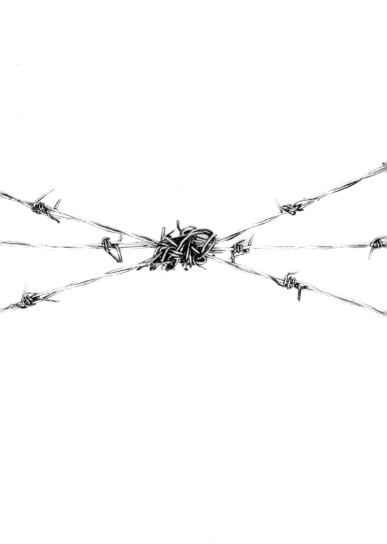

4 Reduce stress instantly

The good thing about stress is that you can always do something about it straightaway. Whether you are encountering aggression at work or coping with sudden and unanticipated problems, you are rarely in a position either to hit out (fight), or to turn on your heels and run (flight). But even when it is a case of 'what cannot be cured must be endured', you can find many ways of releasing those pervasive chemicals which are so damaging to your system.

No matter how much stress has built up, there is always some way you can reduce it. But remember, you do not want to lose all stress, or 'arousal', altogether or you might never get up in the morning.

Use stress busters

Simple physical movement is an excellent way to relieve or alleviate tension immediately. Here are three tried and tested remedies which can be done anywhere. It's a good ideas to try to do them several times a day.

- **Drop your shoulders** Sit up straight, raise your shoulders, and then drop them. This relaxes the muscles which in physical terms means you are not able to take flight, and therefore convinces your body for a few seconds that you are not under threat.

- **Breathe deeply** Put your feet flat on the floor, rest your hands in your lap, drop your shoulders, shut your eyes, and take a deep breath by inhaling through the nose to a slow count of four, and exhaling through the mouth to a slow count of four. This gets the oxygen into the bloodstream via the lungs and back to the brain which helps to clear your mind and enables you to function properly. Do it four times. Start now: one – two – three – four...
- **Move around** Get up and stretch, make a cup of tea, go and wash your hands, pop outside on an errand or just to look at the weather. This improves your circulation and eases tension in your muscles.

With all these actions, movement is the crucial bit. This is a miniature form of fight and flight. Shifting the focus of your mind from what is 'threatening' gives you mental relief and consequently some physical reprieve from your system's 'battle stations'. Once your body begins to calm down, your stomach muscles relax, your digestive system starts working properly and your heartbeat slows, so you automatically feel less tense. This, together with the fact that the brain is getting more oxygen, will help you begin to think more rationally.

Once you have started to think clearly, you will gain perspective and find that what was originally stressing you may not now seem quite so stressful.

Improve your work surroundings

Think about the way you work and consider whether it is work itself that may be increasing your stress levels, or whether it is your stress which is dictating the way you work. Whatever the origin of your stress, there are a number of practical things you can do to improve your situation, such as:

- **Change your working area** If your working conditions are dreary, consider placing plants appropriately, removing mess, and creating a little corner of harmony for yourself. If you haven't got a view from a window, hang up a picture or a poster, even a postcard, of a scene with a perspective, because your eyes are best at rest when looking into the long distance.
- **Have a good clear out** If you seem to lose a piece of paper the moment you put it down, rid yourself of your clutter. If files have not been used lately, archive them, or more radically, shred them and dispose of them. If they are in current use, weed out what is unnecessary to keep. The very act of throwing things away is cathartic. When your surroundings are no longer in a muddle, your mind will find it easy to follow suit.
- **Get organised** If you can keep track of the deadlines you need to achieve, say on a wall chart or in your diary, this will help to eliminate that gnawing sense of helplessness which accompanies your feelings of not

being in control, not being able to find things easily or forgetting appointments.

- **Fix things** If you have equipment that does not perform as it should, get it repaired or but a new one. Fixing the photocopying machine that keeps getting jammed, or the shelf that wobbles, will make you feel you have achieved something concrete, especially when you next come to use it. And when things work properly and no longer cause you frustration, your stress levels also decrease dramatically.

All of these are simple remedies, but none of them is trivial in their impact. It is surprising how being able to find something quickly, or working with equipment that functions effectively, or looking at something restful can reduce a great deal of the stress inherent in your working environment.

Learn to relax

By developing the ability to relax, you actively engage your parasympathetic nervous system, the one which restores energy and makes you feel good.

Watching television is one way to do this, but it is a passive activity. A better way of relaxing is the deliberate unwinding of mental and physical tension when you are completely at rest. The sorts of things you might do might do are:

- **Read a book** This could be a thriller, 19th-century classic, biography, traveller's tale, anything which transports you from the stresses and strains of your daily life into a distant world far removed from your own.
- **Play a tape or CD** Choose something you enjoy listening to. Perhaps something soothing which helps you feel serene and peaceful.
- **Get ourself ready for a good night's sleep** Before you go to sleep, tense, then relax. Separate parts of your body: first your feet, then your legs, abdomen, chest, hands, arms, neck, shoulders, and finally your face. This releases the tension bound up in your muscles and induces a state of physical tranquility.

In addition to your own efforts, treatments provided by professionals can further the process of helping you to relax and feel better in yourself. For example:

- Aromatherapy which involves massage with fragrant oils that relieve tension.
- Deep-muscle massage which comprises kneading the body to promote better circulation, suppleness and ultimately relaxation.
- Reflexology which entails massage of the soles of the feet, providing a soothing hands-on treatment and a personal space in which to relax.

Engaging in various methods of relaxation by yourself or putting yourself into skilled hands to reduce tension helps you become calm. This produces a sense of psychological well-being, renewing your energy levels so that you can tackle your sources of stress positively.

Adopt immediate antidotes to stress

Reducing stress means knowing how to lower your stress levels on a regular basis, so that they do not get out of hand. This need not be a lone effort. You can enlist the help of others to help you relax and feel better, but best of all you now have the means to establish a programme of your own to ease your mind and body.

Having something peaceful to look at provides you with the opportunity to day-dream for a few moments so that you can return to your work invigorated. Improving your working environment means that you will be able to find that vital piece of paper without getting furious or frustrated. Deliberately relaxing your mind and body before you go to sleep lessens the tensions that have been accumulated during the day.

Once you have experienced the rejuvenating effects of short-term remedies, it will encourage you to develop more permanent ways of reducing stress.

Questions to ask yourself

Think about ways of reducing stress instantly and answer the following questions:

- Am I determined to do something about my stress levels straight away?

- Am I prepared to try simple physical movement to reduce tension?

- Am I motivated to organise myself better?

- Do I appreciate how much working with non-functioning equipment can cause me stress?

- Am I resolved to improve my working methods and my surroundings?

- Do I appreciate that deliberately relaxing my mind and muscles before sleeping will lessen the tensions that have accumulated during the day?

You will be doing better if…

- You understand that doing something to reduce stress levels is always better than doing nothing.

- You try 'instant' stress-reducing remedies right away.

- You are encouraged to do something positive to improve the surroundings in which you work.

- You realise that having equipment in proper working order contributes hugely in reducing stress levels.

- You understand the importance of physical movement in lessening your feelings of tension and stress.

- You appreciate that learning to relax can significantly lower your stress levels.

5 Reduce stress permanently

To help yourself manage your stress in a permanent way, you need to take a look at your lifestyle along with your own experience, and use your findings to develop long-term strategies for reducing your stress.

Learn healthy habits

Consider the life you are currently leading and reflect whether it might be contributing to your stress levels, or whether stress itself is affecting your life. For instance, living for your work means you have only the work to focus on and, if it is not going well, any stress you are experiencing has no possibility of being relieved.

To help defuse stress, you need to ensure you are not compounding any bad habits generated by stress. Some key things you need to do are to:

● **Keep to regular sleeping hours** It may be that stress-induced fatigue is exacerbated by a lack of sleep. The simple solution is to get an adequate amount. Late nights or early starts often become routine and may be depleting your energies. You can break the old pattern by having one exceedingly late night and then start as you mean to go on by establishing a new pattern of seven to eight hours of sleep, which will provide the means to allow the body to rest and recoup.

- **Eat healthy food** Stressful eating of snatched snacks can only lead to more stress. The quick boost they give is followed by being left even hungrier than before. The recipe is to take at least 10 minutes to sit down and take time to eat, not a packet of crisps, but a salad or tuna sandwich, preferably away from your work-station. Give your body a chance to digest the food and absorb the nourishment it requires to perform well.
- **Drink in moderation** *(if you want to)* A little alcohol can help you relax and unwind. Too much, though, can act as the fuel which can turn stress into anxiety and depression and worse.
- **Foster personal interests** Being engrossed by something other than work stimulates your mind. And this recharges your batteries and then on your return to work, you can often find answers to things that have been worrying and stressing you.
- **Socialise, or not** If you are an out-going person, fraternising with people, expressing opinions and exchanging ideas can have a restorative effect. It puts stress on hold and problems into perspective. And if you are a more inward-looking individual, taking a break from the hurly-burly by spending time quietly enjoying your own company can rebuild your composure. Choosing an appropriate strategy for you allows your energy levels to revive and this in turn causes you to feel rejuvenated and more able to cope with stress.

By changing the bad habits caused by stress you will begin to realise that you can run your own life, rather than letting your life run you.

Take proper exercise

However much the mere thought of exercise makes you want to lie down, it is an absolutely guaranteed way to reduce stress. Lethargy breeds lethargy. Taking exercise makes you feel energetic because it helps your body to rid itself of those harmful stress-related hormones. Exercise also assists in the production of endorphins which give you a great sense of well-being. You may find it difficult to believe, but once you begin to exercise you will become invigorated by it. But, being 'on the go' all the time is not proper exercise. It has to be the running, cycling, stretching kind to have the right result.

If part of your reluctance towards exercise comes from feeling that you might be wasting your time, use your personal stereo to provide mental stimulus at the same time, and thus kill two birds with one stone. Pick a form of exercise which suits you as this lessens the chance of your giving it up. For example, you could:

- **Walk briskly for 20 minutes each day** Apart from the good it will do you, you will also take in details of surroundings which you would never see from a bus, train or car.

- **Dig out your old bicycle or acquire a new one** Enjoy the exhilaration of travelling under your own steam.
- **Buy an exercise video** You can do a work-out at a time when it suits you and you need not feel self-conscious.
- **Join a sports club** Take up aerobics, swimming or maybe a physical training programme, if you tend to be a more sociable type.

Exercise may initially seem a less attractive course of action but you need to realise it is essential to your well-being. If a hairy mammoth came at you, you would engage in exercise without a second thought. Think of everyday stress as your hairy mammoth.

Use your experience

If you are stressed, trying out new things can seem daunting so you tend to carry on in the same old way.

As the proverb goes: *'If you always do what you have always done, you will always get what you always got.'* Think about your experience and what you have learned from it. Then try to apply what you already know and think about how you might be able to:

- **Recognise your limits** You probably know from painful experience what can and cannot be done, so setting realistic targets will make things look a lot more tangible and achievable.

- **Face up to change** You know when methods are cumbersome or obsolete, and that however tedious the process, changing them will make your life easier and less stressful.
- **Say no** You are usually aware when you might be taking on too much. If you can refuse to do something which you know will cause you stress, this is a sensible course of action, however hard others try to persuade you otherwise.
- **Accept your shortcomings** You know there is no such thing as being perfect, so by recognising that there are some areas where you have shortcomings and admitting to them means that you put yourself under a lot less strain.
- **Avoid certain people** You probably know which people tend to upset you, so if you can make sure that you see them less often, they will be less likely to upset you.
- **Size up a situation** Your experience will tell you if a certain course of action is likely to be stressful, so trusting your instincts as to whether or not to get involved may save you a lot of heartache.
- **Allow time** You know the feeling of panic caused by nearly missing a train or only just making a deadline. Allowing time to buy a newspaper at the station rather than leaping into a moving carriage, and getting ahead of yourself instead of leaving things till the last minute, is infinitely less stressful.

By applying the lessons you have learned from the past you can avoid stressful situations. Don't be wise after the event. You need to recognise that you have considerably greater powers of controlling your world than you think.

Develop strategies for coping

When you get stressed, you tend not to be able to think as rationally as you usually do. This means that you are less able to cope with your worries in a constructive way. The way round this dilemma is to try to address your worries in a methodical manner. This will not only help you to cope, but also will make it far less likely that you become stressed in the first place. There are some practical strategies you can adopt:

- **Decide whether what is worrying you is something you can do something about right now, or not** If there is nothing you can do today, just stop fretting. Put it firmly out of your mind until tomorrow, when you can give it time.
- **Get things into proportion** Rate your worry on a scale of 0 to 10, where 10 is a life-threatening event or illness. You may think it is a big worry, but when you come to rate it, just how worrying is it?
- **Clear your mind** Visualise something calming and peaceful, like a still pond, an azure sky, or a place. This evokes good memories and where no worries intruded

on your pleasure. This stops your mind racing, at least for the few moments needed to bring rational thought to bear.

- **Isolate your worry** Concentrate exclusively on what needs to be done to sort this one, rather than worry about all your concerns together. Say to yourself *'I'm not going to think of anything else but this particular worry.'* This allows you to focus properly on what you can do to resolve the worry. You will then find it easier to work out a number of different ways in which the worry may be resolved.
- **Take a 'helicopter' view** Imagine yourself looking down on the worry from above. Or try imagining that your worry is someone else's worry. This helps to detach your thinking processes and prevents them from being scrambled by your emotions.
- **Get to the heart of the worry** Ask yourself *'What is the real issue here?'* For instance, if you are dreading an early morning meeting, it may be that it is not the meeting itself that is the real worry, but the fact that your alarm clock is unreliable. So get yourself a new one.

If you can develop some or all of these strategies to help you deal with your worries rather than allowing yourself to feel continuously under pressure, you will be constantly lessening the pressure you feel you are under, and this in turn will lessen your stress.

Achieve a balance

If you can establish a balance between your work and personal interests, as well as living a healthy life, you can alleviate much of the stress you may be experiencing.

Stress does not arrive on its own, it has a history. So when facing a new situation you can usually draw on your existing experience and use it to good effect.

Eating proper food, taking energetic exercise on a regular basis, along with developing strategies for coping with worries, are all powerful strategies which will have an appreciable effect on lowering your stress levels.

All these measures provide you with practical ways to reduce your stress on a permanent basis, enabling you to live an emotionally more rewarding life.

Questions to ask yourself

Think about how you might go about reducing stress permanently and answer the following questions:

- Have I identified any ingrained bad habits which I need to change?

- Am I determined to reduce my stress levels by taking proper exercise, now that I know how important it is?

- Do I see that reflecting on my own experience can help me to manage my stress better?

- Do I appreciate that I can readily develop a methodical way to cope with my worries?

- Do I realise that standing back from my worries makes it much easier to identify and resolve the real issue?

- Do I now understand that there are long-lasting strategies for combating stress which are relatively straightforward to implement?

You will be doing better if…

- You resolve to change those habits which are preventing you from living a healthy and fulfilled life.

- You choose the form of physical exercise which most suits you, and keep on doing it.

- You apply your hard-gained experience to prevent yourself from becoming embroiled in predictably stressful situations.

- You develop a constructive and practical approach for coping with your worries.

- You shelve any worry that you can do nothing to resolve at this moment and tackle it on another day when you have more time and space to think about it.

- You promise yourself to keep practising stress-reducing methods so that they eventually become an integral part of your life.

6 Handle stress positively

Understanding the effects of stress is one thing; learning how to handle it is another. But knowing how to put the two together does not necessarily mean you will do it unless your thoughts and feelings go hand in glove with your actions. Unfortunately, it can often be very difficult to adopt a positive approach when you are feeling stressed. Not only do things tend to get out of focus, but negative thoughts are usually predominant.

It is therefore a good idea periodically to re-establish a positive view of yourself and reassert your values.

Verify the good

To regenerate positive feelings, carry out an audit on yourself. By doing this, you can confirm your personal attributes and qualities and verify the good things about your life. The vital areas to consider include:

- **Your goals** Remind yourself of your goals, what you want to achieve. You are more than likely to find that you are pretty well still on track and heading in your chosen direction. By reaffirming your aims, you renew your sense of purpose.
- **Your achievements** Trace your achievements by considering what you have done and identify what you are most proud of. You will be impressed by what you

have achieved. Your recognition of what you have already accomplished should encourage you to believe that you can continue doing so.

- **Your expectations** Check your personal standards against those of others. You will probably find that what you expect of yourself and your performance is a great deal higher than that which many other people expect of themselves. By living up to your standards, you have the reassurance that you know you are doing as a good job as you can.
- **Your strengths** Assess yourself in terms of what you are good at. You are likely to find that you are better at more things than you thought. By appreciating your strengths, you will gain in self-confidence which is a great stress reducer.

The result of this personal audit is far more powerful than you perhaps expected. It will provide you with considerable encouragement to keep going and help you in your quest to achieve your aims.

Adjust your perceptions

Experiments have been undertaken where people were given an injection of adrenaline, the major stress hormone that is produced when you are under stress. This caused them to feel the expected physiological reactions, such as a quickening heartbeat, etc., but as there was nothing to be worried about, no psychological reactions, such as dread, fear or apprehension, were experienced.

This indicates that it is only when people perceive themselves to be under pressure that stress results. It is their state of mind which causes the physiological and emotional reactions, rather than the other way around.

Unfortunately, the instinctive thing is to respond to negative feelings without realising that it is your underlying thoughts which have provoked the response in the first place.

So, for example, when collaborating with a difficult colleague, if you think *'This person is impossible to work with'* or *'Whatever I do, it's never right for X'* you will feel antagonistic so your response is likely to be an aggressive one.

The key to preventing hostile feelings from developing is to change the way you think, known as your cognitive processes. When thoughts are positive, feelings tend to follow suit and lead to responses which are more likely to prevent stress from being experienced. With a difficult colleague, you would therefore:

- **Think** *'X is very good on the technical side of the job, even if he is short-tempered.'* This enables you to decide to...
- **Feel** neutral towards him, which in turn leads you to...
- **Respond** in a very focused way by getting the task done and not engaging in chit-chat.

By making a positive effort to control your initial thoughts, you can engage in a powerful process which prevents adverse emotions from arising. And at the end of the task, you will be surprised by how much you were able to achieve without becoming upset or irritated. This may even result in your considering that working with 'X' was not so bad after all.

When you do not view a situation as being 'threatening', you do not flick the mental switch which prepares your body for the fight or flight response which trigger feelings of apprehension. So stress is kept at bay.

Embrace the locus of control

People who believe that they are in more or less in command of their own actions usually perceive their lives to be less stressful than those who think the outside world is in charge. This concept is called the 'locus of control'.

If you have an internal 'locus of control', you tend to believe that you are master of what happens to you and will willingly take responsibility for yourself and your actions. If, on the other hand, you have an external locus, you are more likely to believe that your life is controlled by exterior forces.

It is important to realise that you play a big part in your own destiny and that it is this which determines your core attitudes to coping with stress. If you are convinced that you control your circumstances, you are far less likely to succumb to the pressures felt by those who believe that circumstances are controlling them. The more you remind yourself that it is completely within you to control what happens to you, the less likely you are to feel like a leaf being tossed about by a storm.

Thinking of yourself as being at the mercy of the elements induces stress, whereas thinking of yourself as always being able to cope with any storm or upset that comes your way is a great reducer of stress.

Choose to take charge of yourself

When you adopt a positive approach to your life and work, you change how you view yourself and how you view stressful situations.

By refusing to let negative thoughts dictate how you are going to feel, and therefore behave, you will find yourself with the power to take charge of your life along with the confidence to do so.

It is important to appreciate that you have far more choice over the way you feel than you realise. Believing that you have control over yourself and are able to take charge of most events you are likely to encounter goes a long way to ensuring that you will effectively handle your stress.

Questions to ask yourself

Think about how you view stress and answer the following questions:

- Have I reminded myself lately of my overall goals?

- Have I recently considered my achievements and evaluated them?

- Do I recognise that I probably perform better than a great many others?

- Do I appreciate the extent of my personal strengths?

- Do I understand that a negative state of mind produces the negative reactions which activate stress?

- Do I accept that positive thoughts lead to positive behaviour which makes many situations seem far less stressful?

- Do I believe that I am in control of my own fate?

You will be doing better if…

- You keep your overall goals in mind and review them regularly.

- You recognise and acknowledge your achievements.

- You reassure yourself that you are doing as well, if not better, than many other people.

- You remind yourself from time to time of your personal strengths.

- You make an effort to change your negative thoughts into positive ones.

- You are convinced that it is you, and only you, who can control what happens to you.

- You know that by adopting a positive approach you will handle stress better.

Check your progress

Should you find that your efforts to handle stress are not working as quite well as you expected, consider whether this is maybe because you may have neglected to take account of one or more of the following aspects.

Understand stress

If you feel tetchier and more miserable than usual, you may not have realised that this could be a result of stress. You may be finding it less easy to think straight or react rationally because you body thinks it is under siege and has prepared itself for battle. This means that you are all geared up to attack or cut and run, but are usually unable to do either. Understanding that there are both physical and mental forces at play can help to explain why you could be feeling under excessive pressure.

Pinpoint stressors

If you are blaming yourself for not coping with various difficulties, it may be that you have skipped the process of pinpointing where your stress is coming from. Perhaps the need to cope with changing circumstances is at the root of your stress. Maybe you are pushing yourself too hard. Or it could be that you have not made enough allowances for the sheer number of worries and problems you have to cope with all at once.

Reduce stress instantly

Should bouts of tension and anxiety be disrupting your work, it is possible that you are forgetting to try simple stress-busting techniques. Or you may not be properly organised so you cannot find things easily. Perhaps you have no calming vista to look at when you need a mental escape from your surroundings. Or you may not be remembering to make time to do some relaxation before you go to sleep.

Reduce stress permanently

If your stress continues to be a persistent presence, perhaps you have not quite got round to putting the major stress-alleviating formulas into practice. Maybe you tried them, but did not persevere. Perhaps you are not be taking sufficient exercise to rid your body of unused stress hormones. Or you may even have slipped back into unhealthy habits.

Your approach to stress

If you feel events are taking you over, it could be that you do not fully accept that it is you who are in charge of your stress. By remembering that it is the way you perceive situations and interpret them that sets up a stress spiral, you can break the sequence. But, above all, it is only when you truly believe that by taking a positive approach to stress, that this will make all the difference in handling stress successfully.

Reap the benefits

Stress is an everyday part of life and once you understand its nature, as well as identifying its causes, you can take positive steps to counteract it.

Being able to handle stress positively has wide-ranging benefits:

- You feel more energetic and enthusiastic about your life and work.
- You are able to think more clearly and logically.
- You are less likely to get exhausted or upset.
- You look and feel better.
- You are more productive and often more creative.
- You are more able to keep yourself calm and regenerate your inner reserves.
- You know there is always something that you can do to help yourself to reduce stress.

Knowing that you can control your stress and that it need not control you is a great relief. It also makes life a great deal more enjoyable and worthwhile.

However stressed you are, once you start practising stress-reducing techniques, you will immediately feel the beneficial effects on your life and performance. All it needs is the will to begin.

Glossary

Here are some definitions in relation to how you can handle your stress.

Anxiety

A lurking dread that something nasty is about to happen.

Balance

A state of equilibrium which is the antidote to stress.

Burnout

An extreme state of mental and physical exhaustion induced by stress. All ash, no spark.

Cognitive Processes

The initial thoughts which influence feelings which in turn influence behaviour. It's all in the mind.

Coping

Being able to keep up with demands.

Depression

The feeling of being in a dark tunnel with no light, no end in sight and with no energy to enable you to escape.

Intrinsic Drivers

Internal compulsions which determine the way you do things. Fine, until they get out of hand.

Exercise

Deliberate exertion. The single most effective way of reducing stress.

Fight or flight

Primitive reactions to fear which remain the body's response to threat, real or imagined.

Hypothalamus

The 'stress centre' in the brain which regulates the body's balance.

Locus of Control

The degree to which people believe they are masters of their own fate.

Parasympathetic nervous system

The body's equivalent of a cup of hot tea and a blanket.

Negative strategies

Ineffective methods for coping with stress which result in your doing all the wrong things.

Positive approach

Believing that good things will happen in your life and yourself.

Stress

Mental and physical pressure resulting in an inability to cope, and made worse by that inability.

Stressor

Anything which causes you stress, from queues to corrupt computers.

Sympathetic nervous system

The body's equivalent of a regiment of artillery, fired up and ready for action.

Further reading

Handle stress provides you with an overview of the basic skills you need to develop to help you reduce your stress levels, think more clearly, along with enjoying life better.

Below are some other resources which you might find useful when developing ways of handling your stress proactively.

Edward A. Charlesworth and Ronald G. Nathan (1997)
Stress Management: *A Comprehensive Guide to Wellness*, New York: Ballantine Books.

Mike Clayton (2011)
Brilliant Stress Management: *How to Manage Stress in Any Situation* (Brilliant Lifeskills), Harlow: Pearson Education Limited.

Sarah Edelman (2006)
Change Your Thinking with CBT: *Overcome Stress, Combat Anxiety and Improve Your Life*, London: Vermillion.

Martin. E. P. Seligman (2011)
Flourish: *A New Understanding of Happiness and Well-Being – and How To Achieve Them*, London: Nicholas Brealy.

About the author

Kate Keenan, CPsychol, AFBPsS, BA, BSc, MSc, MPhil, has over 20 years experience as a chartered psychologist and is expert in the areas of occupational and organisational psychology. Kate specialises in promoting psychological well-being in the workplace. She has worked extensively with corporate and independent businesses, devising strategic management programmes that enable them to identify and resolve managerial issues – from personnel selection and individual assessment to team building and attitude surveys.

She also works as a mentor and coach, offering a series of practical and transformative evidence-based strategies designed to help people make the most of their opportunities, both business and personal. In particular, she helps entrepreneurs and business owners maximise their prime asset – themselves.

Kate has a post-graduate qualification in Mental Health Studies from Kings College, London and currently lives in Bath.

In terms of being able to **handle** her own **stress**, she says:

Being an expert in analysing the causes of stress means that I'm better at helping others to handle their stress than I am at handling my own. However, writing this book has provoked a long overdue impetus to practice what I preach – starting with relaxing my shoulders and taking four deep breaths.'

The Pocket Manager Series

'Especially for people who neither have the time nor the inclination for ploughing through the normal tomes...'

The Daily Telegraph

Personal wellbeing

- Manage yourself
- Make time
- Assert yourself
- Handle stress

Essential business skills

- Plan
- Solve problems
- Communicate
- Negotiate
- Run meetings

Effective leadership

- Manage
- Recruit
- Motivate
- Delegate
- Understand people

More information about these books available at...
www.pocketmanagerbooks.com

To download your FREE Workbook
which accompanies **Handle stress**

please visit:

**www.pocketmanagerbooks.com/books/
handle-stress**

Printed in Great Britain
by Amazon